On Playing With Fire

Athena Tanti

BookLeaf Publishing

India | USA | UK

Presentation by *BookLeaf Publishing*

Web: www.bookleafpub.com

E-mail: info@bookleafpub.com

ISBN: 9789357447058

First edition 2022

DEDICATION

To Nathan.

I love you.

Far more than I hate you.

...

Marriage is hard, ya'll.

PREFACE

There isn't a topic much more narcissistic than myself.
There isn't a form much more pretentious than poetry.
So why have I written this?
Shared experiences is what draws connections with people. I'm trying to connect. I'm trying to show that one is not alone in thought. I'm showing a vulnerabe side to a hardened world in the hopes that it might bridge your humanity to mine. It might be just one poem. Just one line. Or the whole GD book.

Step 1

the blank page, my foe;
until words are formed on thee
broken is your curse

Beginning. Middle. End

I know a girl who reads the endings to the books she reads first. If it doesn't end the way she wants she will not read it. You see, every story has a beginning, a middle, and an end – not always in that order – and she will not read a book she deems sad or doesn't "end" the way she wants it to.

But … does any story end the way you want it to?

On page one we meet a girl, just a girl like any other – she has something unique about her but that's just like any other, right? She has lips that curl at the edges with a crooked smile and we cannot help but fall in love with the freckled fictional face we have created.

In the last chapter, number thirty-eight, the tall man in the long white coat presses a button, and the machine that is breathing for her grinds to a halt, he waits and records the time and walks out of the small halogen lit room – leaving her there with her freckles that have faded into her wrinkly face and her lips that no longer curl at the edges.

I know a girl who reads the endings to the books she reads first. With eager eyes and an anxious heart she double-checks for hurt and heartbreak as the faith she puts in the black and white on paper flutters like a plastic bag in the breeze.

On page 38 she falls and breaks her arm – a man in a long white coat puts a cornflower blue cast on it, but she really wanted the periwinkle red. Later, on page 67 the author uses a clever analogy when she falls in love and the heartbreak is described using the periwinkle red and the cornflower blue. On the last page he described how her once periwinkle red lips – the ones that no longer curl up at the edges – fade to a cornflower blue.

This is a beautiful analogy that is missed by the girl that never read middle because she read the ending to the book first and deemed it unworthy as it may taint her own self.

Every story has a beginning, a middle, and an end – not always in that order – and in chapter twenty-six she gives birth to a happy and beautiful girl who gets freckles, and when she grows up her lips curl just like her mothers when she smirks at the guys that get her attention.

In the next twelve chapters she raises the child on her own showing her what real love is – up until her last dying breath she loved that child and poured herself into her baby girl.

I know a girl who only reads happy books with endings she wants to read. The fictional stories that contain pain are too much for her soul to bear – so she flicks to the end of this book and discovers its sad ending and decided never to read the story.

We are all stories with a beginning, a middle, and an end – not always in that order.

We all meet somewhere in the middle, maybe for a page, maybe for a chapter, but when you come to the girl whose smile is just like her mothers when she looks at a boy she likes and tells sad stories from a sad life – maybe even in poetic form - and you make a judgment based on what is at that middle at that time. Remember once upon a time there was a beginning and there will be an ending and it will be sad but

only because of the beauty that was the middle
and those that made it with her.

I know a girl who reads the endings to the books
she reads first. If it doesn't end the way she
wants she will not read it.

But … does every story end the way you want it
to?

the things I told him before living with me

I keep my clothes on the floordrobe.
I watch far too much Netflix.
I'll sometimes have ice cream for breakfast and
cereal for dinner.

Bin nights are Wednesday. I tend to forget.
The toilet roll faces the person, not the wall.
Clean dishes on the left. Dirty on the right.

I like to cook but hate the clean-up.
I won't always wash my dishes but I'll rinse
them and come back later.
I sometimes forget to brush my teeth.

I bake amazing gluten-free banana bread
but I'll probably eat most of it before you get
home.
I am not a "morning person" until the last
mouthful of my first coffee.

Your happiness is of utmost importance.
And I'll promise to look after me too.
I love you,
I love you,
and I love you.

Who I Am

I am a reflection of me.
Of words I never said but you seemed to hear.
Of misinterpretations and inflections that are
inflicted upon the page.
I am the curve of your smile and the salt in your
tears.
I see myself with the value he places upon me
- which is not much more than a body with parts.

I am what I eat;
which is only what you feed me.
Through failed plans
and broken promises.
I am who you say I am,
sweetheart
darling,
sexy.
Bitch.
Whore.
Skank.

I never asked you to define me
but I find myself in these reflections
in the way you treat me,
in the words you say.

Which says just as much about me as it does
you.

I am what I see
in gloss,
on billboards,
on TV.
Or more, I am what I'm not
In gloss,
on billboards
on TV.
I am a reflection of me.

Aviation 2017

You said you can't wait to read happier poems
about love,
but the feeling of love is nothing but bad
analogies and corny cliches.

I'm on a plane that's taking me away from you,
humans are not designed to fly so high.

The souls of my feet are built for the mud and
dirt
but here we are flying above the marshmallow
clouds
and as we fly through pockets of air pressure we
bump around in our seat belts
with nothing but trust for the pilot and plane.

While my body is in his hands my heart is in
yours
as love is nothing but bad analogies and corny
cliches.

On Discovering Oceans

To all the men who have loved me;
I'm sorry if I never believed you.

My own insecurities suffocate even the purest of
emotion,
swallow it whole, and shit it out; leaving a mess
for someone to step in later.

If I ever said it back chances are I meant it,
but the truth is loving is different from being in
love.

All I've ever done is dip a toe and thought I was
drowning.

To all the men whose lips have met mine;
Thank you.
If only for the second, as saints hands do touch,
you made me feel something.

To the man I kiss,
I hold

I dive into.

I'm sorry.

I have let others love me, and,
I have loved.

I forget, sometimes, that you will catch me.
As I catch you.

Stop struggling and you'll float.
Or drown.

Being loved is not the same thing as loving.
When you fall in love, it is discovering the
ocean
After years of puddle jumping.
It is realising you have hands
- 'No matter the Wreckage' by Sarah Kay

Faye, I miss you

You were so human.
And you showed us what it meant to be human.

You taught us Brecht.
Beckett.
The Effect of Gamma Rays on
Man-in-the-Moon Marigolds.

It means whatever you think it means.

You wrote a play on death.
A lady debates, and contemplates.
She got angry.
She was funny.
She was you.

But we didn't know that.
You didn't know that.

And you fought.
Tooth and nail
until your hair fell out.

I'm sorry I never came to see you.
I had a memory of you that was ...

perfect. In all your imperfections.

I tried.
But she drank.
A lot.
And lied
even more.
And I hope your daughter has grown up to be
half as beautiful as you were.

Because the world needs more yous.
And who you were.
Perfectly human.

Birds

Growing up galahs were my favorite.
Maybe because they were pink
or the way they run
or that they always looked so happy.

We had many birds growing up.
Mother kept letting them out of their cage
to see if they would return.
They never did.

They have personalities, you know
and memories.
And they'll teach others how to treat you.
They think corvidae are sentient,
so they choose who to hate
and know they've chosen.

I keep my birds in a cage now
to protect them from the cats
the foxes, other birds.
It's just too dangerous.

I understand what that means now.
2020. 2021.

Confined. Unable to fly.

Black Kites circle my haven
looking for scraps.
They're huge. They're not afraid.

Swallows annoy my chickens
steal their food
but swoop at the Kites when they come too
close.

I get gallahs in the front yard.
They always look so happy.
I think they're still my favorite.

Workplace training

[Hebrews 12:14]

You keep telling me I have low standards.
I do not understand
the finer things
or how to
do my job.

[Galatians 6:9]

You keep telling me I am not worth what you
pay.
I do not help the team
I do not see
what is around me
and what to do.

[Proverbs 21:25]

It seems like
we both speak English
but the words
have different meanings
like a Paul Jennings story.

[Psalm 56:5]

Put your head up
you told me
for you are a strong
woman
in leadership.

[Deuteronomy 31:6]

But I am not dumb.
I know exactly
who told you
lies
to save themselves.
Their reputation.

[James 4:11]

They poisoned your mind
and now their words
come out of your mouth.

[Proverbs 17:9]

I did not add fuel
to the fire
by bad-mouthing

how they do things
or the goings-on
under the table
or how much
they shoot fire
from their mouths
when they talk about people.

[Proverbs 10:18]

The promises they broke.

[Proverbs 11:18]

Head down, and shy,
with low standards
is not how any person
that actually knows me
would describe me.

[Joshua 1:9]

Outspoken.
Intelligent.
Strong.

[Exodus 15:2]

I dare you to get to know me.

Before you tell me who I am.
Because I do not spit hate
or condemn
or pretend to be righteous.
For I am human.
And I will show you all
you are wrong.

[Psalm 139:14]

A Place For Us

"It's the artists' job to show people the world
they live in. We hold up mirrors."
- Neil Gaiman

The world
closed its doors
March 2020.

My neighbor,
the entertainer,
broke his rib
because he was skyping
a show
from his house
and fell off his unicycle
in the bath.

My tribe,
back home,
the ones who play
with fire
could not make rent
and now meet
under a bridge.

My friends
who write
went into their cave
and came out
with publishing deals
and mental health conditions.

The artist
wonders what's the point
if people can't go
to a gallery.
Is it art
if it can not be seen?
If it doesn't
say something
to someone.

We all sat
and wondered
what's the point
when it is
the artists' job
to show the people
the world
they live in.
We hold up mirrors.

But the only mirror
is our own

fucking reflection
because
the doors are closed
and we can't come out
and we are so sick
of ourselves.

What do we create then?

Left Behind

24

I tap my fingers on the keys
a symbol makes meanings upon a screen
I pause and on a bended knee
illustrate a colour never seen
gambling the reader establishes meaning.

Sanctuary

From this square
of cut out earth
the stars can be seen
and they shine
so bright
the world fades away.

On this mound
when the sun sets
the view through the window
looks like a painting
by Frederick McCubbin
of untamed Aussie bushland.

Out the back
the cows roam,
the sheep meander,
and a miniature pony
named Geoffrey
waits for carrots.

Thousands of flowers
say g'day
when the sun shines bright
and the bees

spend their day
gathering nectar
for their queen.

It's quiet
other than the birds
tweeting, cawing, squawking,
screeching, whistle, and trilling.
At six o'clock
the neighbor rings
an old school bell
to call her children to dinner.

It's a sanctuary
for the soul.
Where nature
is nurtured.
It's not much.
But best of all.
It's mine.

Thank you

Thank you
for listening
even if
you don't always hear
what I say.

Thank you
for telling me
I'm beautiful
almost every day
even though
I don't listen.

Thank you
for staying
when you want to leave
when I see red
and say things
that I don't mean.

Thank you
for choosing me
yesterday
and every day.

Step 2

have something to say
always stand up for something
worthy to be heard.

Dear Dee

Dear Dee,

You can fuck off.

I find everything you do disgusting and it needs to stop.

You snuck into our lives like smoke through the crack at the bottom of the closed door. You entered our houses uninvited and left your filthy fingerprints over everything that was so clean and polished and in its rightful place. Now every picture refuses to hang straight, every locked door still feels unsafe, and every buzz of my phone makes my heart stop out of fear because of you.

I'm sick of how unpredictable you can be. I think the world is fine and then I hear you're talking to yet another friend of mine and I know there's nothing I can do about it because I can't stop; they are their own people.

I'm sick of your addictive personality.

I see it you know. The way you hurt them; the
ones you have touched. How helpless you make
them feel. How I wish I could scream at you to
leave them alone but I know it won't change
anything.

I hate how tightly you've wound yourself around
some of the people I care about most. How
you're squeezing them ever so gently so they do
not feel it until they're already suffocating.

So I wait for you to leave.

But you never truly leave, do you? You've left
your mark like a calling card and cut a hole
where you sit and feel at home.

I'm telling you now you can sit over there; in
your corner staring at me with those eyes. I am
stronger than you know and I refuse to let you
in. You are not welcome in this place.

But sometimes you come in anyway.

I hate how you make us give of ourselves to you.
Like we owe you something. I hate how you
make us feel guilty to give of ourselves to others
and to accept from others.

I wish I could tell people how to not listen to your voice. To not play your games. To free themselves from you.

I hate how you make us feel guilty to give of ourselves to others and prevent us from accepting when others give of themselves.

Instead, I help them recognise you for what you are.

A liar.

I could beg of you to leave my friends alone, but that's not enough.

So, Depression, fuck off.

Yours truly,

Athena.

Things I need to tell myself are not analogies for my heart

I cannot stop the waves from reaching the shore.
I know, I've tried.
Through building deep pits for it to fall
Or walls for it to crash against.
It rises and falls and destroys everything
And yet it keeps coming back for more.

I cannot walk on my hands.
I know, I've tried.
I can gain momentum, and flip upside down
But my hands will not both let me fall
And catch me.
Let me fall
And catch me.
Instead I crumple like a used can
Or tip sideways like a tree
With limbs going every which way.

Every time I fail
I try again until it hurts too much.

I cannot sing a beautiful song
Like, Lana, Amy, or Sia.
I know, I've tried.
I can pluck the strings,
Bang the drums,
Learn the song.
But cannot sing along.

On the stair

There
  on the stair
  with golden hair
she sat.
And waited.

Un-aware of their glare
  she sat on the stair
  with feet bare
  and soles black like despair.
She played with a tear
  her dress in disrepair
  from wear
  and a stain right there
  from using a stair
  as a chair.
She sat.
And waited.
She had no fare
  for the train to St Clare
  and on the stair below her pair
  of filthy feet sat
  a hat
  with a little cardboard sign.
It declared with a dare;

"don't just say a prayer
when life's unfair,
we can't compare
our worth so please give care."

But the millionaire
  and billionaire
  continued up the stair
  nose in the air
  toward The Square
  past the girl with golden hair.

She sat.
And waited.

Man

He was created
with bigger hands
because I always need
something carried.

He is taller
so that when we hug
his head is on mine
and I can melt
into him.

He is stronger
but only uses his strength
when I am not strong
enough.

He is patient
whereas I
was an only grandchild
for twenty-one years.

He is smart
in ways I am not
and I love to listen
and learn.

Unless I am hungry.
Or need coffee.
Which is most of the time.

He does what he can
which some days
is not much
and others
it's everything.

He loves
more than deserving
more than needed
more than wanted some days.

One Picture

I have but one picture of my mother.
One picture that I look at on a somewhat regular
basis anyway.
It hangs in my kitchen. It belongs there.

Not to say that all mothers should be in the
kitchen;
it's a coincidence.

It's not in my bedroom for that is a place for the
happy things
and it's not in the living room
because, well, that is a place for visitors.

This picture is sacred to my soul and is not to be
shared with the common caller.

So in the kitchen she sits, looking at me with
those eyes. Eyes that stare at me in the mirror.
Hazel eyes.
My eyes.
Our eyes.
Our genes.
Shared genes.

Loeys Dietz.
Bad connective tissue.
Shared genes.
Of course, at the time, we did not know this.
That diagnosis came but a decade later. But here
I am, almost her age when she died. With the
same genes.

For the ten years before the diagnosis, I thought
I might have killed my mother.
The stress her body had when carrying me
within her tore a hole deep down inside.
Holes that would have appeared eventually
anyway
like a rotting plastic bag on the inside barely
holding all its contents.
It only takes one tear.
One hole.
Insides on the outsides and all over the floor.
Liquids and solids all mixed.
Broken.

So as it turns out I did not kill my mother.
But now I live with the daily fear that thanks to
genetics she might have killed me.

I have but one picture of my mother.
I yelled at it once.

At sixteen and newly kicked out of home, I was
angry.
I was angry that I thought I killed her. I was
angry that she had let me.
I was angry that she left me in this world
without her.

I tore the picture off the kitchen wall and
slammed it to the floor screaming at her for all
her misgivings.
The glass did not break.
She laid there.
Looking at me with my own eyes.
Smirking during the golden hour.
I grabbed a bicycle pump and with all my might
I repetitively pounded down on the picture until
glass was everywhere.
Why was a bicycle pump in my kitchen?
Shards of glass all over my kitchen floor in no
discernible pattern.
Razor-sharp shards.
Everywhere.
Shards that cut.

As time faded on the scars dissolved back into
my body as I have found new and better ways of
coping with an ever-evaporating life.
The scars on the picture remain.

Little white scratches where the glass shattered
from impact forever haunt me on her chin.
Despite these scars, she smiles at me anyway.
Smiling as though there is no pain and
everything is okay.

I have but one picture of my mother.
It was the last picture ever taken of her.

Overnight at Nanna's.
Phone rings.
        "Your mum's gone to the hospital."
With those words I knew. Even though she was
still alive for two more days I knew.
No more hugs.
No more hellos, goodbyes, goodnights.
No more I love yous.
No more mum.

I knew it was the end.
And the beginning.

At the hospital, we would talk to her
unconscious body.
She might have heard us, she might not have.
But we spoke to her anyway.
I don't remember saying anything in particular.

Other than good-bye.

I hugged her once.
Her formally warming embrace was now still and unresponsive. So I curled in tighter and placed my head on her chest.
I listened to her heartbeat.
Thanks to a mechanical valve replacement her heart used to sound like a ticking clock.
Tick.
Tick.
Tick.
Steady and rhythmic.

But her heart sounded like a timer running out.
Loud in my little ear like a jackhammer.
Time ticking away too fast.

I still can't listen to a ticking clock.
Tear them down, take out the batteries and hide them away.

The next time I saw her she was wearing too much makeup and in a dress I had never seen her wear.
She laid there in a beautiful wooden box; eyes closed, arms crossed.
But it wasn't her.
She wasn't there.
That was a shell; that was not my mother.

Which is perhaps not what I should have
proclaimed when her father kissed her.
But I didn't know how to behave.
Especially not in those white tights that were
rather uncomfortable and made me itch.

After the funeral I was given a picture of my
mother.
A beautiful picture of her.
The sun was setting behind the photographer so
it's full of beautiful orange hues that illuminate a
setting sun's darkening world.
She smiles like everything's going to be okay.
And she looks up at the lens with love in her
hazel eyes.
It was the last picture ever taken of her.

It hangs on my kitchen wall.
It belongs there.

Step 3

believe in yourself
stand up and be strong
create and be seen.

On listening

The thing about pen to paper
(or fingers to keys)
Is that it puts you out there
to judge as they please

It makes one naked
be it heart, mind, soul
And acceptance is sought
whilst one loses control

The reader interprets
whatever they will
and skews the painting
from one's quill

It's hard, dear reader,
to find the words
So that one has said
what is to be heard

So listen, and hard,
to the beat of your heart.
It means what you want
It's abstract art.